How the World Began

Fiona MacDonald

Illustrated by
Emma Shaw-Smith
Yannick Robert
David Eaton
Scott Plumbe

CONTENTS

Dear Reader,

For thousands of years, people have asked: *How did the world begin? Who created it? Who made the first humans?* People in different parts of the world have suggested many different answers.

Some answers come from religious beliefs. Others come from traditional stories, myths and legends.

In this book, I have retold some of these creation stories in my own way. I chose them because I liked them. I hope that you enjoy them too.

Fiona MacDonald

Pan Gu and the Egg

A myth from China

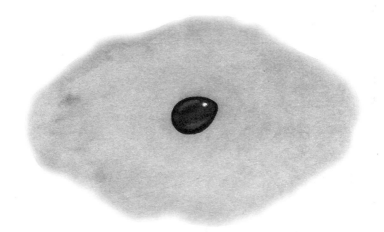

 Way back, in the beginning, there was nothing. Nothing at all. No day or night. No sun or moon. No earth, no sky, no land, no sea.

Just nothing, with the tiniest, faintest, feeblest dot of darkness in the middle. Unless you looked very carefully, you couldn't see it at all. But slowly, slow-ly, s-lo-w-l-y, the dot of darkness grew.

It swelled to the size of a fist. Then it puffed up, as big as a football. It spun round and stretched. It grew longer and thinner, getting bigger all the time.

It became a huge, dark egg – still surrounded by nothing.

For a long time – 18,000 years, they say – the egg just stood there. Big and black and perfect. Outside, its dark shiny shell was always the same – cool, smooth and still. But inside? Inside was very different ...

Inside, there was Pan Gu! A giant, huge and hairy, with big sharp horns. After 18,000 years inside the egg, he had a giant-sized headache. His back ached dreadfully. It was so cramped and stuffy, being shut up in that shell, he had to break free.

Pan Gu pushed and heaved and shoved. He huffed and puffed and panted and groaned. He stamped on the bottom of the eggshell with his feet and battered the top with his horns. He punched the sides with his elbows.

At last, with an ear-splitting CRACK, the eggshell split in two.

Brrrh! Pan Gu shivered in the sudden blast of cold, fresh nothingness that swirled in all around him. Ahhh! What a wonderful feeling as he stood tall and stretched his arms high above his head. Ooooh! What a surprise as the top half of the eggshell flew away from his hands, and floated, just touching his finger tips.

Next, Pan Gu stretched his legs, shook his feet, and wiggled his toes. Whoosh! The bottom half of the eggshell dropped away – then rolled itself out in all directions, for miles and miles and miles.

Pan Gu stared up and down, amazed. Above him there was no longer nothing – but the beautiful blue sky. Below him, there was also something new – the dark brown earth and the grey rocky mountains.

All this looked wonderful, but Pan Gu was worried. (Giants often are, even though they are so big and strong.) Here he was – trapped in between these exciting new creations. What should he do?

If Pan Gu moved his feet, the earth might curl up, or roll away out of sight. If he lowered his arms, the sky might come crashing down on his head.

So he did nothing. He just stood there, flattening the earth and holding up the sky, for another 18,000 years.

Even giants get tired, and, at last, Pan Gu could stand no longer. Weak and weary, he slumped to his knees. Then he stretched himself out all over the earth and the mountains.

To his surprise, the sky did not fall, but floated calmly above him. With a long, drowsy sigh, and a little smile to congratulate himself on a job well done, Pan Gu fell asleep – for ever.

Yes, Pan Gu died, but he did not disappear. Instead, his huge, hairy giant's body changed into the world that we see today.

His two bright eyes became the shining sun and moon.

His blood (pale blue, like most giants' blood) became swift-flowing water.

His bones turned into rocks, his veins into roads, and his strong muscles into rich farmland.

His breath became the strong wind, and
his sweat and tears the life-giving rain. And
most amazing of all, the hairs on his body
flew up to the sky, and were changed into
sparkling stars.

Now, when the sun shines and the world is full of joy, people say 'Pan Gu's spirit is happy!' But when Pan Gu's spirit is sad, dark clouds fill the sky, and the world is miserable, too.

Some people even say that all the fleas and lice on Pan Gu's body turned into the first humans. But that is another story.

Moon and Morning Star

A Native American myth

Long, long ago, when the world was young, everything was fresh and clean. Mountains gleamed white with snow. Trees and grass glowed bright green. Rivers and seas sparkled. Fluffy white clouds floated high in the clear blue sky.

But apart from the Great Spirit, who knew and saw everything, no one could see this wonderful new world because it was always, always, night-time.

The world was strangely quiet, cold, and empty. Nothing moved. Time stood still.

Deep in a cave, a man and woman lay quiet
and still, just like the world around them.
Were they dead? No, but they were sleeping
very deeply. And they were dreaming. They
were the first ever people in the world. Their
names were Man-Who-Brings-Light and
Shining Woman.

At last, they opened their eyes and gazed round their cave, astonished. It was full of everything they had seen in their dreams. What riches! What treasures!

They examined things eagerly, shouting with excitement:

'Look! Stone axes for chopping wood. Bows and arrows for hunting.'

'Look! Flint for making fire and clay pots for cooking.'

'See this! Red earth
for face paint and
feathers for
our hair!'

'Feel this! Soft,
thick, furry animal
skins to keep us
warm and dry!'

'Oh! This is the most
precious gift of
all: a plump golden
corn-cob!'

* * *

Carrying all these gifts from their cave,
Man-Who-Brings-Light and Shining Woman
set out together, to explore the silent world.

As they walked through the shadows,
something startled them. They whispered to
each other: 'What's that, in the darkness, over
there? Oooh! It's moving!'

'Is it a shape? Or a shadow? It can't be a
man or woman like us, but it looks human.'

'Stop! Stay close! I'm frightened!'

The guiding spirit – for that is who it was – stepped towards them, smiling. 'I am Star-Who-Always-Shines,' he said.

'I have left my home in the sky with a message for you from the Great Spirit. He has given you a very important mission – to help the world come alive.'

'I see the future,' Star said. 'I see people and houses, fields and farms. I see laughter and love, quarrels and war. I see hunting, and sports, feasting, singing and dancing. I see life all around us, here on earth. Soon, very soon.

'It is your task to make this future. Now, get busy – begin!' And then Star disappeared.

Man-Who-Brings-Light was the first
to speak.

'Star is right!' he said. 'We must make good
use of the gifts from our dreams, and share
our knowledge. We will have children, to fill
the world with people. We'll help them find
food, and show them how to survive.'

Shining Woman agreed. She showed him
the golden corn-cob. 'With seeds from this,
I will feed everyone.'

They walked on, and with each step, the
chilly darkness vanished. In the east, a bright
glow lit the sky. The sun was rising.

As the sun's rays warmed the earth, trees
shook in the sudden new wind. Rain fell
from scudding clouds; water splashed and
thunder rumbled.

All the birds sang and all the dogs barked;
all the horses galloped wildly. Deep in the
forest, sleepy bears growled, and squirrels
leaped from tree to tree. Eagles soared
overhead. Snakes slithered through the grass.
Even spiders got busy, spinning their webs.
Life was beginning ...

Man-Who-Brings-Light and Shining
Woman travelled through the world until
their children's children's children had grown
up, cleared fields, and built villages. They
showed everyone how to hunt,
fish, cook and play sports
– and plant seeds of
golden corn. They
taught them to care
for each other, too,
to say prayers and
be thankful.

At last, they left this world. But they still watch over it.

On fine nights, we can see them. Shining Woman is now the peaceful, smiling moon. And Man-Who-Brings-Light glows bright and clear as the brilliant Morning Star.

Oran Mor
(The Song of Life)

A Celtic myth

When the world was young, it was a terrible place. Dry as dust. Hard as rock. Hot as fire.

It was torn apart by earthquakes. Ablaze with volcanoes. Seared by lightning. Baked by the fierce glare of the sun. Shivering in the cold, silver moonshine.

It was a dead world. A world without water.

They say the Goddess took pity. Slowly, softly, she scattered the first delicate raindrops. They were a gift, her blessing.

The rain kept on falling, faster and faster, heavier and heavier.

It bounced off the rocks, gushed down the mountain slopes, splashed into puddles, and thundered over waterfalls. It bubbled and babbled in brooks and streams. It raced along in a roaring river.

Rainwater filled the air with mist
and the sky with clouds, while new winds
whispered and whistled. Its spray sparkled
in the sunlight. The first ever rainbows
shone with seven glowing colours.

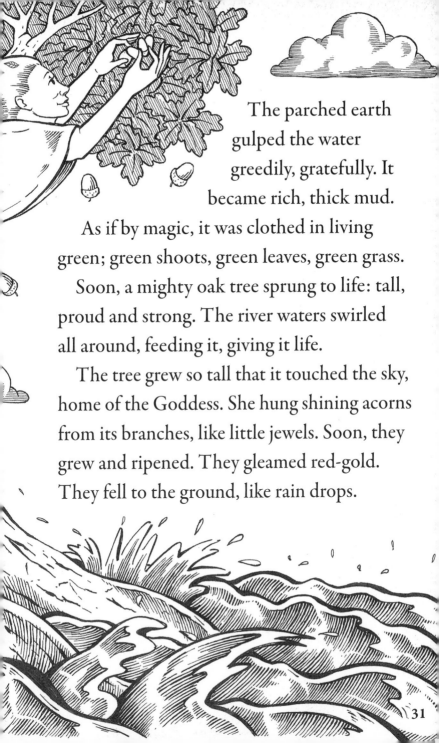

The parched earth
gulped the water
greedily, gratefully. It
became rich, thick mud.

As if by magic, it was clothed in living
green; green shoots, green leaves, green grass.

Soon, a mighty oak tree sprung to life: tall,
proud and strong. The river waters swirled
all around, feeding it, giving it life.

The tree grew so tall that it touched the sky,
home of the Goddess. She hung shining acorns
from its branches, like little jewels. Soon, they
grew and ripened. They gleamed red-gold.
They fell to the ground, like rain drops.

Like the rain, the acorns had magic powers to create, to transform. As they touched the ground, they turned into Daghda (The Good God) and Boann (River Spirit). Together, as the Goddess told them, they filled the earth with people.

• *Boann:* (say) 'boo-an.' • *Daghda:* (say) 'dah-duh.'

The Goddess was generous. Her rain fell
on and on, day by day, year by year. It created
wide rivers, deep dark lakes, and the rough,
restless sea.

Far out at sea, the grey waves rolled and surged. A storm was brewing! Huge walls of water heaved up towards the sky then crashed down, roaring. Fierce winds whipped the water into wild white crests; salt spray screamed through the air.

All day and all night, wind and waves clung together, swirling and swaying in a frantic dance.

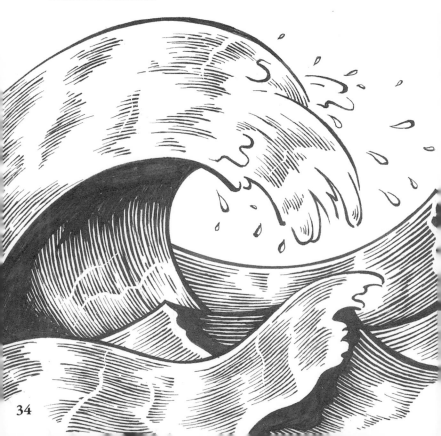

But listen! Can you hear? The storm has blown over. The dance is slowing down. Now, the waves roll to a calm, steady beat, and the wind is sighing. Its voice rises and falls, rises and falls, gently ... gently ... it joins with the soothing sound of falling rain. Its sigh becomes a song.

At first, the song is very, very quiet. But soon it grows louder and louder. At last, it fills the whole wide world with joy, with love, with power.

* * *

They say that we still hear the song – The Song of Life – when the wind blows through the trees, or when the rain patters on the ground, or the waves splash on the beaches.

They say you can hear it in your own heartbeat, and when your friends smile and say hello.

They also say that every time we dance or sing, we create our own Great Song. Our music brings the world new hope, new life, new energy.

Tagaloa's Rock

A myth from Samoa, in
the South Pacific

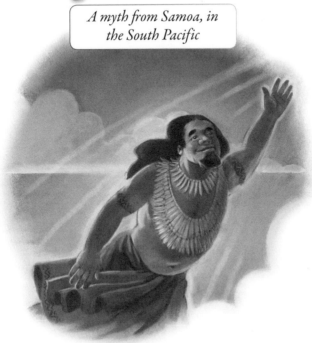

Tagaloa made the sky. It was high
and wide, bright and clear. 'I like it!'
said Tagaloa.

Tagaloa made the sea. It was deep and
dark, mighty and mysterious. 'Amazing!'
said Tagaloa.

Tagaloa soared through the air, flying up,
up, up to see more.

• *Tagaloa:* (say) 'tag-uh-low-ah.' **37**

Tagaloa swam through the sea, diving down, down, down to explore.

Tagaloa was pleased with the world he had made: 'It's wonderful!' he said.

At last, Tagaloa wanted to rest. He could not fly and dive for ever. Where could he stand, or sit, or lie down? There was nowhere.

So Tagaloa summoned up all his energy. With a fearsome frown he gave a giant cry – LAAAAAAAAAAND! – and forced solid rock to heave itself up from the depths of the ocean.

LAAAAND!

At first, the rock was smoking hot. Foul-smelling gases swirled round it. But soon it cooled, and the air around it cleared. Tagaloa nodded, approvingly.

'Ha! The first island in the world,' he said. 'Welcome, dry land, welcome!'

The island was so good that Tagaloa
wanted more. 'I could use them to stride
across the sea,' he said to himself. 'They'd be
like stepping-stones.'

Before long, he'd made them. Hundreds
and hundreds.

A rocky island is a great resting place for a god, but it needs something to cover it. So Tagaloa made green, leafy, creeping plants – and water to keep them growing. With his huge right hand, he smashed into the cliff on the side of his first island.

'Make me a river!' he commanded.

With a deafening CRAAASSSH! the cliff split in two, and cool water came gushing out.

Next – **CRRRUNNCH**, CRRRRACK!
Tagaloa jumped up and down on his island's
highest mountains. 'I'm sorry to squash you,'
he said. 'But I must make some flat land
where my new trees and plants can grow.'

Before long, the flat land was covered in trees and plants. They grew tall, had flowers, and wilted. Then, as their rotten leaves fell to the ground, strange worm-like creatures crawled out of them.

'Ho! What are these?' asked Tagaloa, surprised and very curious. He picked some up, turned them over, and sniffed them, thoughtfully.

'Hmm! Well ... they look interesting. They have definite possibilities. All they need is a head, and two arms, and two legs ...'

Tagaloa got busy.

After a while, he paused, scratched his head, and muttered, 'I must not be too hasty. They will need more than bodies to survive. Now, let me think carefully ...

'Each one must have strength. (I'll put that in their hearts.) And a lively mind. (I'll make sure they've got good brains.) And spirit ... and energy ... I'll give them some of mine! That should help. I'm a god. I have plenty. Then I'll send them all, to live and work and love, on my splendid new rocky islands.'

* * *

And that – so the stories say – is how
the first men and women came to live on
Tagaloa's rock, and all other dry land.

Today, you can still see Tagaloa's islands.
They are far, far away from other countries,
in the middle of the vast Pacific Ocean. You
may have heard some of their names, such as
Samoa, Tonga and Fiji.

Something Special

An Aboriginal myth
from Australia

What would you see if you travelled far
out in space, and looked back towards
planet earth?

Wide seas? Yes! High mountains? Yes!
Green forests? Yes! And vast, empty deserts.

That was what the Brothers saw when they
gazed down from their home among the stars.
The whole earth, spinning in space. Blue,
beautiful – and lonely.

The Brothers were wise, good and kind.
They were also extremely powerful. All day
long, and all night, too, they kept watch over
earth, protecting it.

They saw the sun set and the moon rise.
They saw rainbows, volcanoes, earthquakes.
They saw trees and flowers, animals and
birds. But they couldn't see any humans.

No clever hunters trekked across the
sand or built night-time campfires. No
busy women gathered desert plants, or dug
witchetty grubs to feed their families. No
noisy children ran around, throwing sticks,
chasing dogs, singing songs.

One day, wild winds swirled clouds of
dried-up mud round and round the desert.
As the dust settled, the Brothers gazed down,
watchful as ever.

'What's that, over there behind the rock?
Lurking in the shadows?'

'Just a muddy patch? A little pool?'

'No! Look! It's moving!'

'I can see it! It's moved again! But I think
it's trapped! Is it drowning?'

'We must save it! Quick, Brother! Come with me!'

Like two great birds, the Brothers swooped down to earth.

They hurried to the muddy patch near the rock. They peered at it carefully.

Yes! There was something there, all squelchy and covered with mud, quivering and trembling.

Two Somethings, in fact, side by side. But what on earth were they?

'Here! Scrape the mud away.'

'Lift them up, gently.'

'They're alive, but very weak ...'

'Ooh! They're all wet and slimy.'

'What should we do with them? We can't let them die!'

'You know, I think they might grow and change.'

'I think we should help them.'

Very, very carefully, using their stone knives, the Brothers scraped the mud off the Somethings.

Ah, they were right. Inside each one, they
could just see ... well, what was it?

Gently, they cut round the slimy,
shapeless Somethings. Two heads appeared,
and two bodies.

Slicing deeper, they uncovered arms,
then legs.

The Somethings waved and kicked and
splashed, while the Brothers found their toes
and fingers.

Free at last – and much drier – the
Somethings ran around with glee. But the
Brothers had not yet finished.

'Sit still, little Somethings! Just for a
minute, while we clear the mud from
your faces.'

'There! You each have a nose, eyes, ears
and a mouth. You can speak. You can cry.
You can smile.'

'Now you're Something Special. Yes,
you're ... humans!'